Mentors as Instruments of God's Call

CONTENTS

FOREWORD

■ Mentoring was incorporated into The United Methodist Church in a formal way in 1984, when the General Board of Higher Education and Ministry established a candidacy program to work with persons exploring a call to full-time ministry. At the heart of this program was the naming of a mentor—someone who was trained and equipped to give support and guidance to inquirers as they discerned their call to ministry. In subsequent years, candidacy and clergy mentoring has become a foundational element in the candidacy and provisional programs.

In 1992, the Rev. Justo L. González, a clergy member of the Rio Grande Conference and former professor at Candler School of Theology and the Evangelical Seminary of Puerto Rico, was asked to develop this monograph. Since then it has become a useful resource for mentors and candidates to understand the meaning of discernment as journey, where the mentor accompanies the candidate, walking with him or her in mutual understanding and support.

In the Division of Ordained Ministry's *Fulfilling God's Call: Guidelines for Candidacy,* exploring candidates are invited to recall persons who have shared in (accompanied) or significantly influenced their spiritual journey. *Mentors as Instruments of God's Call* uses Scripture to illustrate such shared journeys. Through biblical narratives, González expounds on many ways and experiences through which God may call persons to ministry. He also invites readers to consider what the Bible may be saying about their particular call.

God uses people to reach other people. González illustrates this through mentoring relationships between several significant biblical characters: Elijah and Elisha—two men with very different personalities, lifestyles, and approaches to ministry; Eli and Samuel—God effectively using Eli as a discerning mentor in spite of his shortcomings; Elizabeth and Mary—Elizabeth being sought out to play a significant role in Mary's discernment at a crucial time in her life; Paul and his many mentors; and Peter—whose response and follow up from strangers impacted the course of his ministry. Each narrative is followed by thought-provoking questions for reflection.

This thoughtful resource, *Mentors as Instruments of God's Call*, augments individual candidacy journeys and conference candidacy programs. It is also a helpful guide for identifying and training candidacy mentors. ▨

Sharon Rubey
Director, Candidacy and Conference Relations
General Board of Higher Education and Ministry
The United Methodist Church
Summer 2009

PREFACE

As we look at the history of the church, it is surprising to note that, of all the various ways in which people have been prepared for ministry through the centuries, none has been as constant as mentoring. Indeed, during most of the life of the church, there were no seminaries; and the few schools of theology in medieval universities were not intended to prepare people for ministry but for academic research, debate, and reflection. Although the New Testament tells us little about how people were prepared to take positions of leadership in the churches Paul founded, there is little doubt that such people were formed and trained through the mentoring of Paul and others. Slightly later, in the second century, churches elected their bishops or pastors from among their members, and these prospective pastors had to prepare a confession of faith to be approved by their colleagues in nearby churches.

How were these people trained? Certainly not in seminaries or universities. There were indeed some schools for the study of Scripture and Christian theology in places such as Alexandria and Caesarea, but only a fraction of the leadership of the church ever attended such schools. The truth is that the vast majority of prospective leaders in the church were formed through the mentoring of other individuals or of the congregation as a whole. When Ambrose was elected bishop of Milan, he called on his former teacher Simplicianus to tutor him in theology. Augustine was already a philosopher and theologian when Bishop Valerius of Hippo practically forced him to become first a priest and then a bishop. From that point on, under the guidance of Valerius and the rest of the church, he learned his pastoral duties and developed a theology that related more directly to those duties. With some variations, most Christian leaders were formed and trained by mentors until the time of the Reformation, when Protestants began encouraging prospective pastors to study at the universities; and the Roman Catholic Council of Trent did likewise, developing the entire system of seminaries which, with significant adjustments, still stands. Thus, seminaries and schools for the formation of pastors, although certainly important, have not always existed; and when they have existed, their academic work has been complemented by a wide variety of forms of mentoring.

For this reason, when we speak today of the importance of mentoring for the formation of Christian leaders for the task of ministry, we should not be surprised. Mentoring is not new. It has always played an important role in the development of new leadership for the church. This is why The United Methodist Church—like many others—stresses the importance of mentoring as part of the formation of Christians for ministry. The reason mentoring sometimes appears new to us may well be that in recent decades we have paid little attention to it, placing the responsibility for the formation of ministerial leadership almost exclusively on institutions, boards, and committees. While all these are valuable and important, their existence does not relieve the church as a whole of its mentoring task.

How was it possible in the second century for a church simply to elect one from among its members as its pastor or bishop, and have that person's theology ratified by the rest of the church? *Simply because the church as a whole was a mentoring community.* Long before they were elected, these prospective leaders were being mentored by individual members in their faith community as well as by the church at large.

There is no more urgent matter for the church today than the need to become once again a mentoring community. The church can no longer count on the surrounding culture to mold the Christian character and to develop the thinking of its members—much less of those who are to take positions of leadership.

It was for this reason that, when invited by the General Board of Higher Education and Ministry in 1992 to produce a booklet on examples of mentoring in Scripture, I was glad to do so. The task set before me at that time was to explore some patterns of mentoring in the Bible, not as an exhaustive list of such patterns but so that we today may see how many forms mentoring takes, and consider how we may be called both to mentor and to be mentored. So, dear reader, it is my hope that, as you read the pages that follow and reflect on the biblical passages, your own calling to mentor, and the manner God may be calling you through mentors around you, may become clearer. So be it! ▪

Justo L. González
Decatur, Georgia
March 2009

CHAPTER 1

MANY CALLS, ONE GOD

■ As you open this booklet, you may be asking, "Am I called by God?" If so, you are asking the wrong question! We are *all* called by God.

First of all, God calls us into existence. In Genesis 1, God creates by calling things out of nonbeing: "God said, 'Let there be. . . .' And it was so" (3-14). And in John 1, we are told that all things have come into being through the Word (1-3)—which means that our very existence is a result of God's Word, of God's calling us into being.

Second, if we are Christians, it is also because God has called us. In Romans 1:6,

Paul refers to his readers, whom he had never met, but who obviously were part of the church, as those "who are called to belong to Jesus Christ." And he also tells his Corinthian readers (many of whom were far from ideal disciples) that they were "called [by God] into the fellowship of his Son, Jesus Christ our Lord" (1 Corinthians 1:9).

But there is a third meaning of the word *call*. This third meaning refers to God's calling us to particular tasks. It is in this sense that we use the word *vocation*, which comes from the Latin for "call." In both epistles quoted above, Paul also says that he is "called to be an apostle" (Romans 1:1; 1 Corinthians 1:1). By this he means that he has received a particular calling, a particular task. If all followers of Christ are such because God has called them, Paul has received, beyond the call to be a disciple, also the call to be an apostle.

We shall be studying something of what the Bible says about the "call" in this third sense. Thus, in a way, this booklet is an invitation to study the Bible. But it is more than that. Our purpose is not to study the Bible in order to understand it better but, rather, to study the Bible in order to understand what God wants us to do. The Bible is "a lamp to my feet and a light to my path" (Psalm 119:105). If we are walking along a path at night, with a flashlight, we make certain that the flashlight shines and that its lens is clear; but rather than looking directly at the flashlight, we use it to illumine the path. The same is true of the Bible. We study it in order to draw its light and to make sure that the lens is clear, but then we must point it at our path so that we may walk without stumbling. Therefore, we shall be studying what the Bible says about the call; but more specifically, every reader is invited to consider what the Bible may be saying about his or her call.

God calls people to different tasks, and therefore the calls are varied in content. You are familiar with the passages in Romans 12:4-8 and 1 Corinthians 12:12-31, where Paul speaks of various tasks in the church as functions assigned to different members of the Body. God calls different people to different tasks. That is how the Body works. Just as no two people are alike, so no two people have exactly the same calling by God. Even in the case of people who have similar calls, there are differences. Paul is an apostle, and Peter is an apostle; but their tasks are not exactly the same. The same is true today. The United Methodist Church, for instance, has different categories whereby it classifies and certifies people for ministry. Some are called into specialized ministries as lay people; some are called into ministry as licensed local pastors; and some are called into ordained ministry as deacons or elders, whose ministries are expressed in many ways within or beyond the local church. Not all have the same gifts nor are called to the same task.

And the calls also vary along the course of an individual's life. Look, for instance, at the story of Paul's conversion in Acts 9. When he asks what he is supposed to do, all that he is told is to get up and enter the city—which, in any case, was what he intended to do before

4

his encounter with the Lord! Then, in Damascus, Ananias comes to him and clarifies the meaning of his vision. (In Acts 9 we are not told that Ananias spoke to Paul of his calling to preach; but in Acts 22:14-16 Paul says that such was indeed the case.) Still, Paul has very little idea what this means, beyond the fact that he is to be a witness. Later, he is preaching near his own native land when Barnabas recruits him to work in Antioch (Acts 11:25). It is in Antioch that he and Barnabas receive the call to set out on a missionary journey (Acts 13:1-3). Along his journeys, there are repeated instances in which God calls him to do things that he did not expect. Then comes the vision of the Macedonian calling him to cross over to Europe (Acts 16:9-10). Each of these is a call from God. All are part of Paul's calling.

This is very important for us to understand as we struggle with the question of our own call. Many who today are considering a call to ministry or a new form of ministry are considering this as a "second career." The same is true of many who are called to the ministry of Word and Sacrament. A woman who spent fifteen years as a teacher, or a man who has been a printer for twelve, suddenly feels compelled to consider a different calling. That does not necessarily mean that they have been doing the wrong thing all along—that they have been disobedient until now. That may or may not be the case. The teacher, for instance, may have decided to become a teacher because she refused to hear God's call; but she may also have been called to be a teacher when she was younger and is now called again to use that experience in a different manner—just as Paul was first called to go to Damascus, then to serve in the church in Antioch, then to become a missionary, and finally to go across to Europe. A new calling does not necessarily nullify the value of the old or of what was accomplished in the past.

There is also variety in the way in which the call of God to specific tasks comes to us. Some calls are quite extraordinary, such as Moses' experience with the burning bush or

Isaiah's vision in the Temple. Others are less spectacular, such as the call to Timothy to join Paul in his ministry (Acts 16:1-5). Yet, no matter how spectacular or how ordinary a call may seem to be, both are equally valid and equally important; for a call derives its value and its importance not from the experience itself but from the Caller, who is none other than God!

Among the many instruments that God uses so that we may hear the call, probably the most important and most common one is another person. Indeed, even in those cases where the most extraordinary experiences are part of the call, we can also discern how God has been using other people to prepare the way for the moment of the dramatic experience. Thus, in the case of Moses, long before the experience of the burning bush, it is clear that God had been preparing Moses for the great task assigned to him. His mother, appointed by Pharaoh's daughter as his wet nurse, kept his contact with the children of Israel. His experience growing up in

Pharaoh's household was also part of his preparation for his task. And the Israelite who was being beaten, and whose plight so provoked Moses that he killed the Egyptian, was at least an instrument preparing Moses for God's call. Later, after the flight from Egypt, his father-in-law Jethro helped him understand and fulfill his new calling as leader of Israel (Exodus 18:13-27). In the New Testament, we have the case of Paul, for it has often been remarked that the martyrdom of Stephen probably prepared the way for Paul's experience on the road to Damascus.

These people whom God uses to help others clarify their call are usually called "mentors." The word *mentor* is derived from the name of Mentor, the unexcelled teacher of Telemachus in Homer's *Odyssey*. It has traditionally referred to a trusted, experienced teacher or guide. In more modern usage, it has become a common way of referring in the business community to someone who "teaches the ropes" to another, and who thus becomes not only a coach but also a sponsor in one's climb along the organizational ladder. There are, however, some differences between all this and what we mean when we speak of a "mentor" who helps us discern the call. They have to do with the differences between the order of the world and the order of the gospel: The purpose of having a mentor is not to assure ourselves of his or her help in a climb up a ladder of power or prestige but, rather, to assure ourselves of having his or her help in listening to what God is calling us to do. And, for similar reasons, the mentors whom we shall be studying are not always exceptional figures in and of themselves but, rather, people whom God chose, sometimes even in spite of their shortcomings, to be instruments of God's call to others.

In the pages that follow, we shall be studying a number of cases in which God used a certain person as an instrument to call others or to clarify their call. Hopefully, you will be thinking about your own call and about persons who have helped or may help you hear that call. Perhaps, you should also be thinking about how you may play a similar role for others by helping them clarify their call. ■

Questions for Reflection and Discussion

1. There are many different callings, all from God. Think about various people in your church and about their different gifts and functions in the church. Is there someone who has a particular gift for organizing people and activities? Is there an "initiator"—someone whose conta gious enthusiasm gets people going? Is there someone who is particularly good at visiting the sick and the bereaved?

2. Remember that God calls people, not only for tasks within the church but also for ministries in the world. As you think about people in your community, can you name some who see their work as a genuine call from God?

miracles done through his hand or any of his harsh words against idolatry and injustice, was the appointment and training of his successor, under God's guidance.

Elijah himself appears in Scripture quite suddenly. We are simply told: "Now Elijah the Tishbite, of Tishbe in Gilead, said to Ahab . . ." (1 Kings 17:1). In contrast to other great personalities of the Bible, we are told nothing of his birth or of his parentage. He simply appears suddenly as a full-blown prophet, challenging the king's idolatry and declaring that there would be a great drought and famine. What we have of him are a series of short stories or episodes. Apparently, he lived in isolation most of the time and came out of the desert only when he had a task to accomplish for the Lord. It is thus that he first appears in the narrative, announcing the great famine to Ahab. He then goes into a sort of exile in Zarephath, a territory belonging to Sidon; and it is there, in the privacy of a widow's house, that two of his most famous miracles take place—the inexhaustible supply of oil and meal from a little jug and a jar, and bringing the widow's son back to life. It is only when the famine has run its course that he returns and presents himself to Ahab, not to announce the end of the drought but to challenge the prophets of Baal and of Asherah. Having defeated them by bringing fire from heaven onto his sacrificial altar, he slays four hundred fifty of them. This provokes the anger of Jezebel, who vows to kill him; and as a result, even after he has announced the end of the drought, he has to flee once again, this time to Mount Horeb. It is there that he receives word from God that he should anoint new kings for Aram and for Israel, and also that "you shall anoint Elisha son of Shaphat of Abel-meholah as prophet in your place" (1 Kings 19:16).

It is at this point that Elisha first appears in the biblical narrative (1 Kings 19:19-21). In contrast to Elijah, we are told more about his background. Elijah finds him plowing, with "twelve yoke of oxen ahead of him, and he was with the twelfth." What this means is that Elisha had a rather successful career ahead of him as a farmer. He was plowing his father's field, not alone but with eleven others, probably servants of his family. He was last so that he could oversee their work. Thus, unlike Elijah, who appears in the biblical narrative seemingly out of nowhere and who led a rather simple life, Elisha is an established young businessman, with connections in the community and a promising economic future.

It was then and there that Elijah "threw his mantle over him." The mantle was both a garment and a sign of office. (Remember the episode in 1 Samuel 24, where David cuts a piece off Saul's mantle, and this is taken as a sign, both that he could have killed the king and that he would be the next king.) Elijah's mantle came to have particular significance. This was the mantle with which he covered his face in the presence of God (1 Kings 19:13) and also the mantle that he would later use to part the waters of the Jordan (2 Kings 2:8). Therefore, by throwing his mantle over Elisha, Elijah was proclaiming him as his successor; and the hymn interprets correctly the significance of this event: "God of the prophets! Bless the prophets' [heirs]; Elijah's mantle o'er Elisha cast."

Elisha has a successful career as a farmer. His response to Elijah's action may be helpful for any who may be considering the possibility of God's call to a new career. He tells Elijah that he must kiss his parents. He must bid farewell properly and leave as a grateful son, not as someone who is running away from failure or from unhappy human relations. Then he tears up his plow and equipment and uses them to build a fire on which to offer his team of oxen as a sacrifice. He is ready to embark on a new life, and he does so both by acknowledging what there was good in the old and by clearly breaking away from it. And yet, even his leaving becomes a feast to which he invites those who used to plow with him.

Elisha followed Elijah for a number of years—probably six or seven. During that time, as was customary in such situations, he acted both as a disciple and as a servant. This is why, when later the king of Israel asks for a prophet, one of his servants answers, "Elisha son of Shaphat, who used to pour water on the hands of Elijah, is here" (2 Kings 3:11). Then Elijah was taken away, and Elisha came to occupy his place.

There are both striking similarities and striking contrasts between these two prophets. The clearest similarities have to do with episodes that seem to parallel each other. Compare, for instance, the story of Elijah and the widow of Zarephath (1 Kings 17:8-16) with the story of Elisha and the prophet's widow (2 Kings 4:17). Note also that both stories are followed by giving a woman a son—in Elijah's case, by raising the widow's son from the dead and in Elisha's by announcing to the Shunammite woman that she would conceive a son, whom Elisha later restores to life.

The differences, however, are even more remarkable. Elijah wore his famous mantle, which apparently was rough; Elisha wore regular clothes. Elijah has traditionally been depicted with flowing long hair; Elisha was bald, and small boys jeered him about it (2 Kings 2:23). While Elijah lived most of the time in the desert and sought human company only when commanded by God to do so, Elisha spent most of his time in the cities or even in his own house in Samaria. Elijah was the dramatic prophet who appeared on the scene suddenly with impressive words and even greater deeds and then apparently retired once again to the desert or into exile. Elisha's ministry covered about half a century of almost constant activity; Elijah's ministry was sporadic. In general, Elijah spoke harsh words, while Elisha was noted for his acts of mercy. Whereas Elijah was feared by Ahab and others in power, Elisha was a trusted advisor to kings, not only of Israel but also of Judah, and even of Moab. Elijah slew the four hundred fifty prophets of Baal; when Naaman tells him that he will have to bow before Rimmon, Elisha responds, "Go in peace." One could say that, although Elijah's was the fiery word of denunciation that clarified the issues, Elisha's was the work of construction that led Israel into new times of obedience.

They were different, partly because their times were different and partly because their backgrounds were different; yet they served the same God. And in this is seen the greatness of both: Elijah's by being ready to appoint as his successor someone who was not very much like him; Elisha's by being able to respond to new challenges in ways that were not mere repetition of what his teacher had done and to learn from someone whose lifestyle was so different from his own. ■

Questions for Reflection and Discussion

1. Elijah was the instrument that God used to call Elisha. Have you ever considered the possibility that God may be using you to call others?

2. Apparently, Elisha was quite content plowing his field until Elijah issued God's call to him. Has anyone ever suggested that God might be calling you to a particular task? Did you take him or her seriously?

3. Elijah was able to name Elisha his successor and to train him, without making Elisha a carbon copy of himself. What do you think it takes for a mentor to be able to do this? Elisha was able to learn from a person whose lifestyle was very different from his own. What do you think it takes for a mentor and a disciple to develop that kind of relationship? Can you point to similar relationships in your own life or in the church?

CHAPTER 3

ELI AND SAMUEL

The story of Eli and Samuel is well known. Yet, we often miss the profound drama involved. Indeed, we tend to think of Eli as a great priest, one of whose many accomplishments was that he trained Samuel. But if you read the biblical account again (1 Samuel 1–4), you will note that, apart from his relationship with Samuel, Eli is a sad figure.

The Bible does not say a word of Eli's accomplishments. We know that he was a priest at Shiloh and that he was a judge of Israel for forty years (1 Samuel 4:18). This joining of two such offices in one person was rather extraordinary. But we are not told that, either as a priest or as a judge, Eli did anything exceptional.

The one thing we know of Eli, apart from the stories connected with Samuel, is that his two sons, Hophni and Phinehas, were scoundrels who "had no regard for the LORD or for the duties of the priests to the people" (1 Samuel 2:12). They took advantage of the sacrifices offered at the altar, taking the best part for themselves; and their sexual mores left much to be desired. All that Eli did was offer them a mild rebuke; and as a result, an unnamed prophet came and told him that because of his sons' behavior, and because of Eli's acquiescence, his sons would die violently; and no longer would his descendants serve as priests of the Lord. It all sounds like the sad but all too common story of a parent whose children are spoiled, with the result that both the parent and the children suffer. At the end of his life, when he was ninety-eight years old, the tragedy unfolded. His sons were killed in a battle in which the ark of God fell into the hands of the Philistines. When Eli heard the news, he fell from his seat by the gate, broke his neck, and died. Yet that was not the end of the tragedy, for his daughter-in-law, Phinehas's widow, went into labor when she heard the news. As she was about to die as a result of childbirth, she gave her son the sad name of Ichabod, which means "inglorious," or "gone is the glory" (1 Samuel 4:10-22).

If we were employing the term *mentor* as it is often used today in the business community—as a sponsor who can help one get ahead in a competitive world—then Eli would be far from filling the bill. There was nothing particularly striking or appealing about him. Measured by standards of success, fame, and glory, he was a loser. It is the story of Samuel that gives luster to Eli's otherwise dull life. Indeed, Eli is remembered as Samuel's mentor, as the one through whom Samuel heard and interpreted his call.

Even in that connection, Eli does not appear as a particularly sensitive or perceptive person. At the very beginning of the story, before Samuel was born, his mother, Hannah, was praying fervently at Shiloh, asking God for a son. When Eli saw her praying so fervently, with her lips moving but without uttering a sound, he thought she was drunk and said to her: "How long will you make a drunken spectacle of yourself? Put away your wine" (1 Samuel 1:14)—certainly not the words of a particularly sensitive priest or pastor! It was then, however, that Eli showed the trait that allowed him to be Samuel's mentor and which made him great in spite of his mediocrity: He was able to see his error and to take a new direction. When Hannah told him that he was wrong, rather than rebuking her further for speaking thus to a person in his position of authority, Eli blessed her: "Go in peace; the God of Israel grant the petition you have made to him" (1 Samuel 1:17). As a result of this, Eli—a mediocre and perhaps even insensitive person—was given the responsibility to raise one of the greatest leaders of Israel, for Hannah promised the child to the Lord. Accordingly, when the child was weaned, she brought him to Eli and said: "I am the woman who was standing here in your presence, praying to the LORD. For this child I prayed; and the LORD has granted me the petition that I made to him. Therefore I have lent him to the LORD; as long as he lives, he is given to the LORD" (1 Samuel 1:26-28).

The Bible says very little about young Samuel's life under the guidance of Eli. Actually, all that it says is that Samuel was "ministering to the LORD under Eli" (1 Samuel 3:1). One can imagine that Eli taught him not only the rituals of the sacrifice but also the traditions of Israel, and most especially who the God of Israel was, and what that God had done in Israel's history. Clearly, if one judges by the results, Eli, who by now was "very old" (1 Samuel 2:22), did a much better job with Samuel than he did with his own two sons.

The other episode that the Bible recounts regarding Eli and Samuel is the call of Samuel. In this regard, you may wish to read 1 Samuel 3. The story, told in brief, is that Samuel heard a voice calling him by name and thought it was Eli, who by now was almost blind. Three times he heard the voice; and three times he ran to Eli, only to be told that Eli had not called him. Here again, Eli appeared slow to realize what was actually happening. By the third time, however, Eli understood and told Samuel that it was the Lord calling so that, if he should hear it again, he should say, "Speak, LORD, for your servant is listening" (1 Samuel 3:9). Samuel did so, and the Lord did speak to him.

It is at this point that the story, as often told in Sunday school, ends. But in the Bible the story goes on. The word from the Lord was dreadful: Eli and his house would be punished for the sins of Eli's sons and because Eli had not restrained them. Quite naturally, Samuel did not wish to tell Eli what the Lord had said. But Eli insisted, and Samuel finally told him. Chastised, and recognizing that what God had said was true, old Eli accepted the divine judgment. He could have discounted what Samuel told him as the musings of an imaginative child. Instead, he said, "It is the LORD; let him do what seems good to him" (1 Samuel 3:18).

As we look at this entire story of Eli and Samuel, thinking in terms of the call and how it comes to us, three elements stand out. First, Eli may not be an outstanding character; and yet God uses him to train Samuel and to help him understand his call. Second, although Eli is a far cry from Elijah, he is quite ready to correct himself when he discovers that Hannah is not drunk, and even to accept God's dreadful judgment when it comes. Third, as in the case of Elijah and Elisha, but even more so, Samuel's task will be widely different from that of his mentor, Eli. This is particularly significant, since Eli, who for all practical purposes had already lost his sons and knew that they were not worthy of following in his footsteps, could have easily been tempted to make Samuel into an extension of his own personality.

Some of the implications for us today should be obvious. As we seek to discover our call, we do not need to find an absolutely outstanding mentor but, rather, one who, even in spite of personal shortcomings, is willing to listen with us for the Word of God and to be obedient to God's will. If, on the other hand, we are called upon to serve as mentors or as guides to others, what is required of us is not that we be outstanding personalities or paragons of virtue but, rather, that we be willing and able to listen with them for the Word of God. And, both for those of us who are placed in the role of serving as mentors and for those of us who are to benefit from such mentoring, it should always be clear that, no matter how much we would like for others to follow in our footsteps or how much we would like to follow in another's footsteps, God will be calling the newer generations to different tasks than the old, as time and circumstances change. ■

Questions for Reflection and Discussion

Think about each of the following possible qualifications in a mentor who could help you discern your call:

- Being a successful example and role model
- Being knowledgeable and professional
- Being open to new possibilities
- Seeking another to continue his or her work
- Having spiritual discernment
- Having similar experiences to yours

Reflect on each of these. How would you rank these qualifications in looking for a guide or a mentor? Are there other qualifications you would add? Are there some in this list that you would consider completely unimportant?

CHAPTER 4

MARY AND ELIZABETH

■ As the basis for this study, you may wish to read Luke 1:5-56. It is a story we have all read repeatedly and have also heard at least once a year, as Christmas approaches. Yet, precisely because we have heard it so often, we easily miss some of its most important and startling points.

Note that the story of the birth of Jesus begins not with him or with his mother but with the story of Zechariah and Elizabeth. If you were a first-century Jew reading this story for the first time, you would have found it quite familiar. Indeed, one of the themes

that appears repeatedly in the Hebrew
Scriptures—what we now call the Old
Testament—is that of the barren woman
who conceives through divine intervention.
In the previous chapter, we came across one
such case: Hannah praying fervently at
Shiloh, after many years of childlessness, and
conceiving Samuel. If you go back to the
Book of Genesis and read the stories of the
"Patriarchs," you will note that Sarah,
Rebekah, and Rachel were all barren until
God intervened (Genesis 15:1-2; 16:1;
17:15-21; 29:31; 30:1-2). This shows, first of
all, that God is interested in the matriarchs as
well as in the patriarchs. Abraham, for
instance, believes that what is important is
for him to have a son. Even Sarah agrees. So
they decide that Abraham will take Hagar
and thus assure a progeny. But God's plan
includes both Abraham and Sarah. In the
case of Hannah's husband, Elkanah, his other
wife, Peninnah, had already given him sons;
but it was from Hannah that the great
prophet Samuel was to be born.

It is for this reason that a first-century Jew would have found the beginning of the story in Luke quite familiar. Elizabeth and her story seem to be the continuation of a pattern clearly established in Jewish history.

Then comes a strange twist in the narrative: Another woman appears in the picture. This one has even more reason to be childless than Sarah, Rachel, or Elizabeth: She is a virgin. Indeed, the text tells us that she is a virgin and unmarried even before it tells us her name. And, just as in the case of those other barren women, Sarah, Hannah, Elizabeth, and the rest, Mary is told that she will conceive and bear a son.

Mary's response is quite understandable: "How can this be, since I am a virgin?" (Luke 1:34). We read these words, having heard them many times and knowing what the rest of the story will be, and therefore miss much of the drama. Put yourself in Mary's place. She is not just asking for an explanation. She is also expressing her perplexity. When you look at it this way, you see the parallelism between Mary's response and Sarah's. Sarah laughed. Mary questioned. What both actions express is the perplexity, wonderment, and even anxiety, brought about by the angel's announcement.

There are, however, some important differences between Mary's story and those of all the barren women in the Old Testament. For them, conceiving and bearing a child w a triumph and a vindication before the rest o. the world. This was something for which they had been yearning. Others saw their barrenness as a sign of God's displeasure. Sometimes they themselves agreed. Therefore, they rejoiced when they conceived.

Mary's case is quite different. She is not even married, and therefore having a child is the last thing on her mind. Furthermore, precisely since she is not married, her pregnancy will not be seen as a vindication but, rather, as a cause for shame. Although Luke does not mention this explicitly, Matthew does. Look at Matthew 1:19. There we are told that Joseph was ready to spare Mary from "public disgrace" and that, therefore, he "planned to dismiss her quietly." In other words, Mary's pregnancy was likely to result in public shame or, at least, in Joseph's rejection. Matthew then goes on to tell us that an angel appeared to Joseph and explained what was happening and that, on that basis, Joseph went ahead with the marriage. Therefore, Mary's question, "How can this be, since I am a virgin?" (Luke 1:34), may well involve a tinge of protest. It is in this light that we must understand the drama of her entire conversation with the angel, and her final words, "[L]et it be with me according to your word" (v. 38).

Then, there is a second difference between Mary's story and those of the other barren women we have met throughout the Old Testament. The angel tells her that she is not entirely alone in her condition. Her cousin Elizabeth has also conceived and is already in her sixth month. Note the contrast between this story and that of Hannah and Peninnah. In that other story, there was rivalry between the two women. Peninnah's children were seen as a further cause for the humiliation of Hannah. Although at first Sarah seemed to have no objection to Hagar's union with Abraham, when she saw the two children playing together, she pressured Abraham to dismiss Hagar and her son (Genesis 21:9-14). And, although Rachel and Leah were sisters, we are told that "when Rachel saw that she bore Jacob no children, she envied her sister" (Gen. 30:1).

In contrast to that attitude, Mary goes to visit Elizabeth. She has learned from the angel that her cousin is pregnant. The news could have been cause for envy and rivalry. After all, Elizabeth's pregnancy would be reason for rejoicing and honor, while Mary's brought her the risk of shame and rejection. It would have been quite understandable if Mary had decided to stay at home and hide her pregnancy. Yet that is not what she does. On the contrary, she goes "with haste" to visit her cousin.

The two pregnant women meet. One is married and six months pregnant after being childless for a long time. The other is also pregnant but probably still unmarried. One might wonder what thoughts went through Mary's mind, as she journeyed into the hill country of Judea, worried about what her cousin might say when she learned of her pregnancy. (Remember, both Elizabeth and Zechariah "were righteous before God" [Luke 1:6]; and all too often the righteous stand ready to judge those who do not meet their standards.)

The meeting of the two women is a cause for rejoicing. Far from being judgmental, the first thing that Elizabeth says to Mary is "Blessed are you among women" (Luke 1:42). From that meeting, Mary draws strength and inspiration, and utters words of praise patterned after Hannah's song many centuries earlier. No matter what the world might think, her pregnancy too is a vindication (vv. 46-48):

> "My soul magnifies the Lord,
>   and my spirit rejoices in God
>   my Savior,

for he has looked with favor on
    the lowliness of his servant.
Surely, from now on all
    generations will call
    me blessed."

Then, at the end of her song, we are told
something that we often miss but that is
quite significant: Mary remained with
Elizabeth three months and then returned
home. By now her pregnancy would be
showing. This would normally be the time of
greatest dread, when people would begin
demanding explanations and making conjec-
tures. Once her pregnancy was that
advanced, we would expect Mary to remain
in the hill country of Judea until she came to
term. But that is not what she does.
Somehow, partly through her visit to
Elizabeth, she has gained the strength to
return home.

All of this is closely related to our sub-
ject. When the angel tells Mary that her
cousin Elizabeth is also pregnant, he is offer-
ing her the opportunity for support in her

difficult situation. The two relatives find themselves in situations that are in some ways similar and in some ways very different. This could have been the occasion for rivalry and alienation from each other, as in the case of Hannah and Peninnah. But that does not happen. Mary goes to visit her relative, who being older, could provide her the support she needs. Elizabeth, on her part, is guided by the Spirit to receive Mary with open arms and a word of blessing. The result is joy and strength for both of them.

In a way, Elizabeth is Mary's forerunner, just as her son John is the forerunner of Mary's son Jesus. Being pregnant as the result of God's activity provides her a point of common experience with Mary. Being older provides her the possibility of supporting and mentoring Mary through her difficult times.

When we speak of mentoring, we are often speaking of people who belong to different generations. One is more experienced than the other. That difference in experience is obviously necessary for genuine mentoring.

They also have some experiences in common. That too is necessary for true mentoring. These commonalities and differences are such that they could easily lead to conflict and rivalry, as was the case between Hannah and Peninnah. Yet, when a spirit of understanding and solidarity prevails, both the differences and the commonalities can be truly affirmed. ▪

Questions for Reflection and Discussion

1. A mentoring relationship is not always easy. The fact that both parties work at similar tasks, and yet one is more experienced than the other, can easily lead to jealousy and rivalry. Can you think of situations in your own life where that has actually happened? What can we do to avoid it?

2. Mary and Elizabeth had much in common: They were relatives; they were women; they were pregnant. There were also differences between them: one young,

the other older; one married, the other probably still single. What do you think are the most important points that people should have in common in order to have a profitable mentoring relationship? What sort of differences should they have?

3. Very often in a mentoring relationship, one party is considerably older than the other. How does that affect the relationship? Does the relationship between Mary and Elizabeth show us something in that regard?

4. If you are already in a mentoring relationship, the two of you may wish to list and discuss what you have in common as well as the differences between you. Are you using both your commonalities and your differences to their highest potential?

CHAPTER 5

PAUL AND HIS MANY MENTORS

■ Although we have already mentioned Paul's call (or, rather, his multiple calls), it will be helpful to study his life in more detail. As we do so, we shall discover that Paul had not one but many mentors. Of these, at least three stand out: Ananias, Barnabas, and the entire church of Antioch. The Bible tells us very little about each of these, and yet it is clear that they all played an important part in Paul's discernment of his call.

Ananias was the very first Christian whom Paul met after his experience on the road to

Damascus. Later, Paul declared that Ananias was "a devout man according to the law and well spoken of by all the Jews living there" (Acts 22:12). This may have been important; for immediately after his experience with the Lord, Paul met a Christian who was also known as a devout Jew and who, therefore, was exceptionally qualified to lead this new convert, who until very recently had been persecuting the church in the name of Judaism. In any case, it was this Ananias who introduced Paul to the Christian faith and invited him to be baptized. He also was the one who first spoke to him of his call to "witness to the world of what you have seen and heard" (Acts 22:15). And, like Eli in his relationship with Samuel, Ananias attained his renown through this relatively brief contact with Paul. (While there are other people in the New Testament who are also called Ananias, they should not be confused with this one. In fact, the Bible mentions this Ananias only in connection with Paul's first contacts with the Christian community in Damascus.)

Then there is Barnabas. We know a bit more about him. His true name was Joseph, and he was a Levite from Cyprus. According to Acts 4:36, he had been named Barnabas by the apostles; and this meant "son of encouragement." In the very next verse, we are told that he sold a field and gave the money to the church, to be distributed by the apostles. He does not appear again until after Paul's conversion, when the disciples in Jerusalem would not allow Paul to join them; for they remembered how he had persecuted the church and were still afraid of him. It was Barnabas who "took him, brought him to the apostles, and described for them how on the road he had seen the Lord, who had spoken to him, and how in Damascus he had spoken boldly in the name of Jesus" (Acts 9:27). So, Barnabas was the mentor and sponsor who introduced Paul to the church in Jerusalem, which would play such an important role in his life.

Later (Acts 11:19-26), Barnabas was sent by the church in Jerusalem to see what was happening in Antioch. When he saw what was taking place in Antioch, "he rejoiced, and he exhorted them all to remain faithful to the Lord with steadfast devotion" (v. 23). Although Acts does not tell us whether Barnabas made a brief trip to Jerusalem to report on his findings, it is clear that Barnabas was so impressed by the church in Antioch that he decided to remain there, serving the Lord in that church. It was then that he "went to Tarsus to look for Saul, and when he had found him, he brought him to Antioch. So it was that for an entire year they met with the church and taught a great many people" (vv. 25-26). In this case again, Barnabas was God's instrument for Paul's call, although now by inviting him to join in the work that was taking place in Antioch. Then, when the time came for what we now call "Paul's first missionary journey," Barnabas seems to have been the real leader of the enterprise in its early stages; for in several of the early episodes of that journey, Barnabas is mentioned before Paul. Later, as they continued their work, Paul came increasingly to the foreground.

Things did not always go well between Paul and Barnabas. At the beginning of their second missionary journey, their ways parted, mostly because they did not see eye to eye as to what was to be done with Mark, Barnabas's nephew, who had abandoned them at the beginning of the first journey and who now wished to join them again (Acts 15:36-39). They also seem to have disagreed about some of the theological issues being debated in the early church (see Galatians 2:13). But in spite of this, Paul always had great respect for this man who had played such an important role in his own call. Indeed, in the Galatians passage, Paul declares his surprise that one of Barnabas's character and stature could have acted as he did: "[A]nd even Barnabas was led astray. . . ." Later, when writing to the Colossians, Paul again had Mark with him and was ready to mention the young man's kinship to Barnabas as a commendation (Colossians 4:10). What is important to remember is that, at more than one point in his life, Paul received guidance from Barnabas.

Finally, there is the group of Christian leaders in Antioch. It was when these five—Barnabas, Simeon Niger, Lucius of Cyrene, Manaen, and Paul—were worshiping the Lord and fasting, that "the Holy Spirit said, 'Set apart for me Barnabas and Saul for the work to which I have called them'" (Acts 13:2).

This was the beginning of Paul's missionary career, which would earn him the title of "Apostle to the Gentiles." It is to be noted, however, that the call to go on a missionary journey did not come to Paul directly and in private. Paul did have other such experiences, such as the call to Macedonia. But in this first missionary calling, the Spirit speaks not to Paul but to the entire group that is worshiping and fasting. In a sense, the group as a whole becomes a mentor through whom Paul (with Barnabas) comes to understand his call more fully.

What all of this means is that Paul did not have one mentor but many. He did not arrive at his missionary vocation by following a role model or by having a great teacher or by purely private inspiration but through the agency of many other Christians. Later, he did have disciples such as Timothy and Titus, whose mentor he was. But he himself, rather than one great mentor, had many. ■

Questions for Reflection and Discussion

1. Among Paul's mentors, Ananias seems to have played a role at the very beginning of his Christian work, and Barnabas at the beginning of his missionary career. Eventually, both Ananias and Barnabas faded into the background. Is this the proper role of a mentor? How does a mentor know when it is time to fade into the background? How do we know when it is time to leave a particular mentor and set out on our own?

2. In the call of Paul and Barnabas to set out as missionaries, the community of faith—or, at least, its leaders—played an important role. It was to them that the Spirit gave instructions to the effect that Barnabas and Saul should be set apart for a particular ministry. Today, the church has structures and procedures whose function is to help determine whether a person has been called by God for a particular, "set apart," ministry. Does this passage help you understand the value and legitimacy of such structures and procedures? What would you say to people who insisted they were called by God to a particular ministry but found no confirmation of that calling in the community of faith? On the positive side, how does God employ the church to help us discover our call?

CHAPTER 6

PETER, JOHN, AND THEIR UNEXPECTED MENTORS

We have studied the manner in which mentoring—by which we mean guidance from others—helped three leaders among the people of God to discern their call. These three leaders were Elisha, Samuel, and Paul. Some of their mentors, such as Elijah and Barnabas, were themselves highly successful and respected. Others are known mostly or only as a result of their mentoring—Eli and Ananias. All of them, however, were active members and even leaders of the people of

God: Elijah was a great prophet; Eli was a priest and judge; Ananias, Barnabas, and the "teachers and prophets" at Antioch were all church leaders.

Yet, God does not always choose church leaders—or even church members—to let us hear our call. Therefore, in this final chapter of our study we shall focus on what could be called "unexpected mentors"—people outside the community of faith who, nevertheless, were instruments whereby Christians discovered added dimensions to their call.

The first two chapters of Acts speak of a time when the church apparently had little conflict with the community around it. It was the time of Pentecost and immediately thereafter; and Acts tells us about the disciples leading a life of intense community, frequent worship, selfless sharing, and unbounded joy. Then, at the beginning of Acts 3, Peter and John went to the Temple as usual at the hour of prayer, when a man who had been lame from birth asked them for alms. Nothing more natural than that; and nothing more natural than for the disciples to answer as Peter did: "I have no silver or gold, but what I have I give you; in the name of Jesus Christ of Nazareth, stand up and walk" (Acts 3:6). We often quote that passage without realizing that it is precisely as a result of these words of Peter, and of the ensuing miracle, that the early community of the disciples found itself in conflict with the authorities of the land and was called to new dimensions of witnessing.

Peter and John thought that they had simply done what was expected of them, and continued on their way to worship. But the man who had been healed would not leave them alone—the Bible says, "[H]e clung to Peter and John" (Acts 3:11). His testimony to what had been done in his life forced the apostles to give further witness, and therefore Peter addressed the multitude in Solomon's Portico. Again, that was simply a continuation of what Peter and others had already done at the day of Pentecost. But the story does not end there. The authorities and civil leaders—"the priests, the captain of the

temple, and the Sadducees" (Acts 4:1)—
arrested Peter and John, kept them in prison
overnight, and the next day took them before
the rulers, elders, and scribes.

The story goes on. You may wish to read
Acts 4:1-31 and 5:12-42. The gist of what
Acts tells us is that, as a result of the healing
of the lame man and of Peter's speech at the
Portico of Solomon, the disciples are ordered
by the Council to remain silent and to teach
no more in the name of Jesus. This command
they obviously cannot obey; and this, in turn,
leads to further clashes with the authorities,
an ever firmer resolve on the part of the disciples, persecution, and the eventual disper-
sion of the disciples, so that the gospel was
carried far and wide. In a way, the spread of
Christianity throughout the world—the very
fact of our being Christians today—stems
from that seemingly minor act of Peter and
John, when they responded to the lame
man's need by healing him.

What this means is that often God calls
us by means of people who are not even part

of the church but whose need itself and our response to it open new avenues for service and Christian growth. Jesus himself said that, when we meet a person's need, we meet Jesus (Matthew 25:34-40). This does not mean simply that we shall be rewarded "as if" we had been serving him. What the text in Matthew actually says is that, in serving such people, we serve Jesus Christ.

There is an old story of a young Christian convert in the fourth century, a soldier whose name was Martin. It is said that one cold winter day, as Martin was entering the city of Amiens, he saw a beggar shivering with cold and asking for alms. Since Martin had no money, he took his cape, tore it in two, and gave half to the beggar. His companions laughed and chided him; but, as the story goes, Martin was more than compensated when he had a vision in which his Lord came to him, wrapped in half a soldier's cloak, and said to him, "[J]ust as you did it to one of the least of these who are members of my family, you did it to me" (Matthew 25:40).

The story may be true or not, but the point that it makes leaves no room for doubt: When Martin gave part of his cape to the beggar, the two were not alone. There was a Third Person with them: the one who had promised, "just as. . . ." In the beggar, Martin met Christ.

So it has been through the centuries, and so it is with us today. God speaks to us, not only through preachers, teachers, other church leaders, and the church itself but also through the needs of the world. We do well to seek mentors among the leaders of the church. But let us not forget that our God has also provided for us other mentors, other instruments through whom we can also hear God's call. And among these unexpected mentors are those around us who may be in need—whatever their need may be. ■

Questions for Reflection and Discussion

1. As you think about your call and look at the world around you, what needs do

you see to which you could help provide an answer? What gifts, experiences, and resources do you have that could help meet those needs? Could it be that the very presence of those needs is a call from God to you?

2. If it is true that God speaks to us through our encounters with the needy, could it be that sometimes our refusal to meet the needy is due, in part, to fear of what God could demand of us? If Peter and John had not healed the lame man, they would have saved themselves a great deal of trouble. Could that be one reason we sometimes try to keep the needy at a distance?